Unveiling the Gospel

Jesus and the Question of Organized Faith

By
Yesu Vi

Copyright 2025 Yesu Vi. All rights reserved.

No part of this book may be reproduced in any form or by any electronic or mechanical means including information storage and retrieval systems, without permission in writing from the author. The only exception is by a reviewer, who may quote short excerpts in a review.

Although the author and publisher have made every effort to ensure that the information in this book was correct at press time, the author and publisher do not assume and hereby disclaim any liability to any party for any loss, damage, or disruption caused by errors or omissions, whether such errors or omissions result from negligence, accident, or any other cause.

This publication is designed to provide accurate and authoritative information with regard to the subject matter covered. It is sold with the understanding that the publisher is not engaged in rendering professional services. If legal advice or other expert assistance is required, the services of a competent professional should be sought.

The fact that an organization or website is referred to in this work as a citation and/or a potential source of further information does not mean that the author or the publisher endorses the information the organization or website may provide or recommendations it may make.

Please remember that Internet websites listed in this work may have changed or disappeared between when this work was written and when it is read.

Unveiling the Gospel

Jesus and the Question of Organized Faith

Table of Contents

Introduction 1

Chapter 1: Contextualizing the Gospel 4
    Understanding the Historical Jesus 4

Chapter 2: Jesus and the Temple 9
    Jesus' Actions in the Temple 9

Chapter 3: The Sermon on the Mount 13
    Teachings on Religious Practices 13

Chapter 4: Parables and Their Meanings 17
    Parables Critiquing Religious Leaders 17

Chapter 5: Encounters with the Pharisees 21
    Analyzing Jesus-Pharisee Dialogues 21

Chapter 6: Jesus' Views on the Law 25
    The Role of Mosaic Law 25

Chapter 7: Community and Fellowship in Jesus' Teachings 29
    Building Spiritual Community 29

Chapter 8: Jesus and Synagogue Practices 34
    Engagement with Synagogues 34

Chapter 9: The Kingdom of God as an Alternative 38
    Vision of the Kingdom 38

Chapter 10: Jesus' Critiques of Religious Hypocrisy 43
    Identifying Hypocrisy in Worship 43

Chapter 11: Sacrifice, Ritual, and Faith 47

Reevaluating Traditional Sacrifices 47

Chapter 12: The Legacy of Jesus and Organized Faith 51
Jesus in Early Christian Thought 51

Conclusion 56

Appendix A: Appendix (if needed) 59
The Historical Context of Jesus' Teachings 59
Interpreting Parables Beyond the Surface 59
The Ongoing Dialogue with Pharisees 60
Reflecting on Spiritual Community 60

Introduction

In the grand tapestry of human history, few figures stand out as vividly as Jesus of Nazareth. His life and teachings have not only shaped religious thought but also left an indelible mark on culture, society, and the nature of belief itself. This book aims to delve into a nuanced aspect of Jesus' legacy: his views on organized religion. In doing so, we embark on a journey that promises to be as enlightening as it is challenging, inviting us to explore the intersection of faith, institution, and individual spirituality.

From the bustling streets of ancient Jerusalem to the quiet corners of Galilean hills, Jesus' message resounded with a profound call for transformation. Yet beyond the miracles and parables lies a critical voice that questioned the established religious norms of his time. Jesus' relationship with organized religion was complex, often contentious, and yet deeply insightful. Understanding this relationship requires us to peel back the layers of tradition and rediscover the radical aspects of his teachings.

The intent of this exploration is not to diminish religious institutions but to encourage a deeper reflection on their roles today. Institutions, by nature, provide structure and community, offering a sense of belonging and continuity. However, they also run the risk of becoming rigid, losing touch with the spiritual essence they once sought to cultivate. Jesus, with his focus on the heart over form, challenged such tendencies, prompting an examination of faith that transcends mere ritual.

To understand Jesus' perspective, it's crucial to immerse ourselves in the world he inhabited—a world teeming with political tension, religious fervor, and social upheaval. The socio-political landscape of first-century Palestine adds layers of richness and complexity to his narrative. Here, emerging sects of Judaism navigated Roman occupation, striving for spiritual and political autonomy. In this setting, Jesus emerged as a catalytic figure, a voice that refused to conform, pushing the boundaries of religious thought and practice.

As we embark on this exploration, it becomes essential to recognize Jesus as more than a distant historical figure. His teachings carry timeless relevance. His critiques of religious hypocrisy, his embrace of marginalized communities, and his vision of the Kingdom of God challenge us to reconsider our assumptions about faith and community. Through these lenses, we perceive organized religion not as an adversary but as a malleable construct—capable of evolving, growing, and most importantly, aligning with the core of Jesus' message.

This book invites you to explore the profound wisdom found within Jesus' interactions with the structures of his day, his revolutionary perspective on religious practices, and his challenges to the status quo. This journey demands openness, a willingness to question, and an eagerness to understand the heart of his message. More than a historical inquiry, this is an exploration into the spiritual, offering insights into how faith can thrive amidst and beyond institutional frameworks.

In approaching this study, keep in mind the varied voices of theologians, historians, and spiritual leaders who have struggled with similar questions across centuries. Their diverse perspectives highlight the layers of meaning embedded in Jesus' critiques and teachings. By considering these interpretations, we enrich our understanding and appreciation of the multifaceted dialogue between Jesus and organized faith.

As we proceed, let us embrace the spirit of inquisitive reflection and transformative learning—a hallmark of Jesus' path. Perhaps in understanding his perspective on organized religion, we may uncover fresh insights into our own beliefs, prompting growth for both the individual and the collective. As we question and seek, may we find not only answers but also a deeper connection to the essence of spiritual life itself.

Chapter 1:
Contextualizing the Gospel

Plunging into the heart of the gospel, we start by painting a vibrant picture of the era in which Jesus lived—a time bursting with spiritual ferment and societal change. This chapter is about peeling back the layers and immersing ourselves in the cultural and religious milieu that shaped the historical Jesus. Walk with us through the dusty streets of first-century Judea, where diverse threads of belief and tradition intertwine to form the backdrop of his message. Understanding Jesus in his historical context is crucial to grasping how his teachings challenged the confines of organized religion, pushing boundaries and inviting transformative contemplation. By exploring this landscape, we aim to unravel the broader narrative and set the stage for a deeper examination of how Jesus' revolutionary ideas intersected with and critiqued institutional faith. Let's embark on this journey, questioning and deciphering how this historical context informs the essence of the gospel, urging a fresh encounter with familiar stories, and inspiring a heartfelt exploration of faith and its practice.

Understanding the Historical Jesus

In the realm of historical inquiry, uncovering the truth about Jesus means sifting through layers of tradition and cultural backdrop to glimpse his reality as a first-century figure. This task isn't just about what he preached but understanding the environment that shaped his perspectives and actions. To truly contextualize the Gospel, one must peek into the socio-political landscape of ancient Judea, where Roman occupation, Jewish tradition, and revolutionary ideas clashed. Jesus emerged not just as a spiritual icon but as a perceptive commentator on the religious mores of his day, critiquing and often reinterpreting established norms. With compassion and wisdom, his teachings carved a path that questioned the rigid structures of organized religion, urging a return to authentic spirituality. By delving into the heart of Jesus' world, we find a compelling tapestry of faith interwoven with the threads of daily life, challenging us to reconsider the true essence of organized belief.

Exploring First-Century Judaism reveals a complex and vibrant world that shaped every aspect of Jesus' life and teachings. In understanding the historical Jesus, it's essential to grasp the rich tapestry of Jewish culture, religion, and politics during the first century. This period was marked by diversity and tension, as various Jewish sects navigated the challenges of Roman occupation and internal strife. The backdrop of first-century Judaism provides critical context for Jesus' message and interactions with religious authorities.

First-century Judaism wasn't monolithic; it was a mosaic of beliefs and practices. Different sects, like the Pharisees, Sadducees, Essenes, and Zealots, coexisted with varying degrees of harmony and conflict. Each group had distinct interpretations of the Torah and traditions, contributing to a dynamic religious atmosphere. For instance, the Pharisees emphasized strict adherence to the Law and oral traditions, which often brought them into conflict with Jesus. Understanding these sects' beliefs helps us decode many of Jesus' interactions and teachings.

Socio-political dynamics were also crucial in shaping the first-century Jewish context. The Roman Empire's control over Judea led to increased taxation, political corruption, and occasional revolts. Many Jews anticipated a Messiah who would liberate them from

Roman oppression, fulfilling the prophecies of old. This expectation of a political savior is vital in understanding the diverse reactions to Jesus, who preached a different kind of kingdom—one not of this world but rooted in spiritual renewal and ethical transformation.

The religious landscape of the time was primarily centered around the Temple in Jerusalem. The Temple was not just a place of worship but a symbol of Jewish identity and God's presence among His people. However, it was also a place rife with political manipulation and economic exploitation. Jesus' actions in the Temple—driving out money changers and traders—can be seen as a direct challenge to these corrupt practices. This act wasn't just about cleansing a sacred space; it was a profound statement against institutionalized religious hypocrisy.

Alongside the Temple's centrality, synagogues played a key role in Jewish religious and social life. These local centers were where communities gathered for prayer, teaching, and fellowship. Jesus often taught in synagogues, engaging directly with the people and challenging them to rethink their understandings of the Law. His interpretations often emphasized compassion over legalism, inviting his listeners to view God's commandments through a lens of love and justice. This fresh perspective resonated with many but also provoked opposition from those committed to traditional practices.

The impact of Hellenism further complicated the Jewish religious experience. Greek culture, philosophy, and language penetrated heavily into Jewish society, influencing everything from literature to religious thought. Some Jewish groups embraced these influences, while others resisted, striving to maintain their distinct identity. This cultural tension is reflected in various scriptural texts and likely in some of Jesus' teachings, which aimed at a deeper, more authentic spirituality.

Exploring first-century Judaism also requires understanding the role of prophecy and apocalyptic literature. Many Jews of the time held a fervent belief in the coming of God's kingdom, a divine intervention that would restore Israel's fortunes. These apocalyptic hopes often featured in Jesus' discourses about the Kingdom of God. By positioning Himself within this narrative, yet redefining it to include themes of inner transformation and repentance, Jesus both challenged and fulfilled prevailing expectations.

In the fabric of first-century Judaism, purity laws and rituals formed an essential thread, guiding daily life and religious practices. Jesus' approach to these laws was revolutionary. He often prioritized human need and compassion over ritual purity, highlighting the spirit of the Law rather than its letter. This perspective encouraged a more inclusive view of community and spirituality, challenging exclusions based on strict interpretations of purity.

Economically, the first century was a time of significant disparity, with a small elite benefiting from Roman rule and the majority living in poverty. Understanding this economic landscape is crucial, as Jesus' teachings frequently addressed issues of wealth, poverty, and social justice. His parables, exhortations to love one's neighbor, and pronouncements about the rich and the poor gained potency in this socio-economic context, advocating for an equitable community living by God's values.

First-century Judaism also witnessed a vibrant oral tradition, with stories, teachings, and debates forming a vital part of cultural life. The oral nature of teaching meant that Jesus' words and stories could be adapted and retold across different contexts, making them both accessible and revolutionary. The parables, sayings, and dialogues attributed to Jesus fit within this oral culture, allowing his message to resonate across various audiences and social strata.

Ultimately, the exploration of first-century Judaism offers a profound understanding of the setting in which Jesus lived and taught. By appreciating the diversity, challenges, and expectations of Jewish life at that time, we gain a richer perspective on how Jesus' message both clashed with and complemented prevailing beliefs. His teachings opened avenues for spiritual and social transformation, challenging his contemporaries to envision a different relationship with God and each other. This historical context is not just a backdrop; it's a key to unlocking the nuances of Jesus' mission and message, a testament to the profound impact he had on shaping religious thought and practice in his era.

Chapter 2:
Jesus and the Temple

Transitioning from the socio-religious backdrop of first-century Judaism, we find Jesus entering the temple—a central symbol of Jewish faith—and revealing a complex relationship with institutional religion. The temple stood not just as a house of worship, but as a cultural and political hub; its grandeur and authority were meant to inspire awe and reverence. Yet, Jesus' actions within these holy walls spoke volumes, challenging the status quo and turning established norms on their head. In this charged environment, he wasn't merely addressing the corruption of religious practices but was also advocating for a profound connection with the divine that transcends physical spaces and structures. Through his radical engagement with the temple, Jesus was urging those around him to look beyond stone and sacrifice, to a faith defined by spirit and intention rather than ritualistic adherence. This pivotal moment invites us to reconsider how we engage with institutional religion, urging a return to faith's essence and reminding us that the true temple is built within the heart. The narrative compels us to ponder: In our own spiritual journeys, where do we draw the line between tradition and genuine connection with the divine?

Jesus' Actions in the Temple

In the bustling heart of Jerusalem, Jesus' actions in the Temple created a stir that rippled across the religious landscape. With eyes blazing and purpose set, he walked into the sacred space and disrupted the norm.

This wasn't just anger; it was a passionate plea for purity, a call to return to the spiritual essence of worship. Amidst the clatter of tables and the surprised gasps of onlookers, Jesus challenged the transactional nature of faith that had taken root. He overturned the tables of money changers, not merely as an act of defiance, but as a vivid illustration of the dissonance between genuine devotion and commodified ritual. By clearing the Temple, Jesus invited a profound reflection on what true worship should be: a heart-centered union with the divine, free from the trappings of commerce and corruption. This moment was more than a protest; it was an invitation to rethink the intersection of faith and institutional practice, urging believers to seek a deeper, more authentic relationship with God.

Interpretations of the Temple Incident offer a multi-faceted window into understanding both the person of Jesus and his perspectives on organized religion. The cleansing of the temple, vividly portrayed in the Gospels, has sparked numerous debates among theologians, historians, and spiritually curious individuals. Why did Jesus choose this moment, this act of defiance, as one of his pivotal public demonstrations? To some, it's a prophetic act, reminiscent of Old Testament prophets like Jeremiah, protesting corruption and calling for a spiritual renewal of Israel. For others, it's a symbolic gesture challenging the commercialization of religious practices.

When Jesus overturned the tables of money changers and drove out those buying and selling, it was a radical statement against the transactional culture that had infiltrated sacred spaces. The temple, a place intended for communion with the divine, had, in Jesus' eyes, become tainted by worldly concerns. This notion echoes his broader message: that divine connection should be unmediated and genuine, free from the constraints and corruption that often accompany institutional religion. It's a call to his followers to look beyond ritualistic practices to find deeper spiritual truths.

Moreover, this incident can be understood within the larger context of Jesus' mission to redefine and deepen spiritual practices. He sought to remind the people of the temple's original purpose—a house of prayer for all nations. This perspective aligns with his other teachings that emphasize sincerity over rites. The temple incident thus serves as an essential critique of religious authorities who had allowed tradition to overshadow the spiritual essence of faith.

The scene in the temple also underscores Jesus' boldness and his willingness to confront the status quo. Not only did he disrupt the activities of the day, but he also provoked the ire of religious leaders, setting the stage for future confrontations. To understand the full significance of this act, one must acknowledge its bravery; it was an unmistakable challenge to an established order that was not easily swayed. Jesus didn't merely voice his disapproval; he enacted it, creating a physical manifestation of his teachings and convictions.

Another interpretation views the temple cleansing as a microcosm of Jesus' broader message regarding the Kingdom of God. This kingdom wasn't about political power or architectural grandeur but about a new spiritual order rooted in justice, righteousness, and genuine worship. By challenging the temple's defilement, Jesus symbolically highlighted the need for a new covenant, one that prioritizes direct and honest engagement with God over cumbersome and often exploitative religious frameworks.

This incident has not only shaped theological studies but also sparked reflections on the nature of religious reform. Many have seen parallels between Jesus' actions and later movements that sought to renew or reform religious institutions. His actions encourage believers throughout history to question practices that deviate from their foundational spiritual goals and to seek reform when rituals become stale or hypocritical. The temple incident urges a proactive stance against religious complacency.

It's also noteworthy to consider the nuanced timing of this event in Jesus' ministry. Occurring near Passover, a time of renewed hope and reflection in Jewish tradition, the temple incident gains further significance. It aligns Jesus' mission with the liberation themes of Passover, drawing a connection between historical deliverance from physical bondage in Egypt and the spiritual liberation he sought to bring. This adds layers to the understanding of Jesus' strategic and symbolic actions.

Finally, the reactions to Jesus' temple cleansing encapsulate the spectrum of responses to his ministry. Some were likely appalled by what they perceived as violent upheaval, while others found hope and a call to spiritual awareness in his actions. The diverse interpretations that emerge from this singular event reflect the broader divisions Jesus often evoked—challenging individuals to reevaluate their understanding of faith, worship, and the nature of religious institutions.

Each interpretation of the temple incident, whether seen as a protest, a prophetic act, or a call to a higher form of worship, converges on a central theme: the pursuit of authenticity in one's spiritual life. Jesus' actions in the temple underscore his relentless passion for faith that transcends form and penetrates to the heart of worship. Through this powerful demonstration, he invites us to question, reflect, and transform on our spiritual journeys.

Chapter 3:
The Sermon on the Mount

In considering the Sermon on the Mount, we find ourselves peering into a wellspring of radically transformative ideas, ones that seem to ripple through time, challenging and reframing the religious understanding of its day. Jesus' discourse, delivered upon that gentle slope, is not merely a moral code or a collection of wise sayings, but rather a profound call to reimagine the essence of true spirituality. Through his vivid teachings, Jesus invites us to transcend the constraints of religious formalism and instead embrace a spirituality rooted in authenticity and love. This sermon, with its timeless beatitudes and admonitions, offers a compelling vision of inner purity, urging each listener to interrogate their motivations and find beauty in humility, mercy, and peacemaking. Here, the boundaries between divine commands and personal transformational goals blur, presenting an opportunity to align personal faith with compassionate action. In doing so, the Sermon on the Mount becomes more than a historical artifact; it's a living dialogue between the soul and a higher purpose, urging believers to walk a path that's vibrant with intention and imbued with the spirit of true righteousness.

Teachings on Religious Practices

In the Sermon on the Mount, Jesus delivers profound insights on religious practices, urging his listeners to transcend mere ritual and embrace genuine spirituality. He emphasizes authenticity over public display, teaching that true communion with the divine isn't about ornate ceremonies or external approval but is found in the sincerity of one's heart. By focusing on acts of righteousness done in quiet and prayer spoken in solitude, Jesus advocates for an intimate relationship with God, one that is untouched by the superficial expectations of the society around him. This paradigm shift challenges the status quo, beckoning followers to re-evaluate the essence of their faith, making it less about ritualistic adherence to tradition and more about cultivating an inner truth and love that transcends beyond structured practices.

Implications for Organized Faith The Sermon on the Mount, with its profound teachings on religious practices, echoes through time as a revolutionary discourse that challenges the very core of organized faith. When Jesus addressed the crowds on that hillside, he wasn't just speaking to the people of his day; he was laying down a blueprint that continues to inspire and provoke thought among spiritually curious minds. His teachings offer a radical reconsideration of what it means to live a life of faith, often in stark contrast with the established practices of organized religious institutions.

It's essential to recognize that the Sermon on the Mount does more than propose personal spiritual ethics; it questions the ostentation often associated with institutionalized religion. Consider when Jesus spoke about prayer, fasting, and almsgiving. He wasn't dismissing these practices altogether, but rather urging a return to authenticity. His words encourage a focus on intent and sincerity over ritualistic observance. For organized faith, this presents a challenge and an opportunity to scrutinize the line where tradition and genuine spirituality intersect.

This reflection prompts organized religions to reevaluate their approaches to worship and religious duties. The heart of Jesus' message lies in fostering an internal transformation rather than a mere external display. Religious institutions, therefore, must navigate the delicate balance between preserving cherished traditions and cultivating authentic spiritual experiences. It's a call for a more intimate, personal faith that prioritizes genuine relationships with the divine, rather than being confined within the walls of customs and dogma.

Furthermore, the emphasis on humility and the condemnation of hypocrisy resonate profoundly within the framework of organized religious structures. Jesus' critique of those who performed religious acts for social recognition challenges these institutions to ensure that their practices do not become mere formalities devoid of true meaning. This is no small task. It requires ongoing reflection and willingness to evolve, as faith communities strive to heed Jesus' call for purity of heart and intention.

In response to these teachings, some religious organizations have embraced reforms aimed at promoting inclusivity and authenticity. By shifting their focus from institutional achievements to the spiritual growth of individual members, they align more closely with the principles Jesus advocated. This transformation, however, isn't without its struggles. The process of reorienting religious practices is complex and requires courage from both leaders and followers to embrace change while honoring sacred traditions.

Yet, Jesus' teachings in the Sermon on the Mount suggest that it is necessary. They call for a faith that transcends the limitations of institutional mindsets by encouraging a humanitarian perspective that cares deeply about others and the world. Organized religions, in essence, are invited to become living embodiments of compassion, mercy, and love—principles that are foundational to their very existence.

It's undeniable that these implications stretch beyond theoretical contemplations into practical applications. Religious authorities must grapple with the societal impact of their doctrines and how they relate to the ethical imperatives presented by Jesus. By prioritizing actions over appearances, as Jesus modeled, religious communities have the potential to transform into pillars of hope and agents of change.

The Sermon on the Mount, thus, serves as both a mirror and a map. It reflects the core of Jesus' teachings back to organized faith, encouraging it to examine itself earnestly. At the same time, it offers a pathway for those institutions to embody the genuine spirituality and ethical integrity that Jesus exemplified. In this light, the teachings continue to evoke a dynamic interaction between personal spirituality and collective religious expression.

Ultimately, the legacy of the Sermon on the Mount in relation to organized faith is one of hope and possibility. By embracing the challenges and opportunities embedded within Jesus' words, these institutions can seek to align themselves more closely with the spiritual ideals he championed. In doing so, they might just find themselves at the forefront of a renewed religious landscape, defined by a sincere commitment to living out the principles of love, humility, and integrity.

Chapter 4:
Parables and Their Meanings

Jesus often chose parables as his way of illuminating profound truths, a method that simultaneously engaged and challenged his listeners. These stories, rich with metaphor and layered meanings, served as a mirror reflecting the virtues and failings of humanity. Through the parables, Jesus critiqued not just individual behavior, but also the broader structures of religious authority. His tales of lost sheep, give-and-take talents, or the persistent widow were more than just moral lessons; they were a subtle rebuke of spiritual complacency among the religious elite. While these leaders clung to laws and rituals, Jesus' parables called for introspection, urging his audience to think beyond the tangible and examine the integrity of their faith. By wrapping radical ideas in simple narratives, he compelled listeners to seek deeper truths, encouraging transformation that starts from within. This method of teaching not only exposed the shortcomings of institutional religion but also offered a vision of a more personal, sincere relationship with the divine.

Parables Critiquing Religious Leaders

In his parables, Jesus frequently aimed a discerning eye at the religious leaders of his time, unveiling the disconnect between their public piety and private practices. These stories are more than simple tales; they are incisive critiques woven with both wit and urgency, driving home the gap between righteous appearance and authentic spirituality. By likening religious figures to unyielding stewards or blind guides, Jesus wasn't merely pointing out their personal flaws but was challenging the very framework of how religion was being practiced and perceived. His parables are vivid illustrations of the human condition, encouraging believers to look past hierarchical positions and question what lies beneath the surface. They're a call to return to genuine faith, contrasting the hubris of the few with the humble heart that seeks God truly. These narratives still resonate, urging us to reflect on our own practices, and reminding us that true spiritual leadership is grounded in selfless service rather than title or tradition.

Responses to Institutional Religion The parables of Jesus, especially those critiquing religious leaders, serve as a mirror reflecting the challenges of institutional religion. In these narratives, Jesus often employs metaphor and narrative to critique the practices and attitudes of those in positions of religious authority. These stories aren't just timeless tales; they're pointed narratives that shed light on the tensions between spiritual authenticity and institutionalized belief systems.

At their core, these parables reveal a deep concern with how religion, when institutionalized, can drift from its intended purpose. Jesus used parables as a means of engaging with the various audiences of His time, delivering complex messages through simple stories. The criticisms embedded within these tales were not merely subtle; they were radical, challenging the status quo and encouraging listeners to reflect critically on their own beliefs and practices.

One such parable is the "Parable of the Good Samaritan." Here, Jesus turns societal expectations on their head by highlighting the compassion of a Samaritan—considered an outsider—over the religious leaders who passed by a man in need. The story questions the integrity of religious leaders who prioritize ritual purity over genuine care. This critique of institutional religion underscores the tendency to elevate form over substance, a theme that echoes through the centuries.

Another example that illustrates this tension is the "Parable of the Pharisee and the Tax Collector." This story is a direct challenge to the self-righteousness that can pervade religious leadership. By contrasting the humble prayer of the tax collector with the boastful prayer of the Pharisee, Jesus questions the sincerity behind the Pharisee's public displays of piety. It's a stark reminder of how easily rituals can morph into performances rather than acts of faith.

The impact of these stories on institutional religion is profound. They invite followers to look beyond the trappings of organized practices and to seek a heart-centered faith. These parables suggest that real spirituality may be obscured by dogma and traditions that fail to reflect the true spirit of the teachings they claim to uphold.

It's worth noting that Jesus did not outright reject institutional religion. Instead, he urged a transformation from within. His criticism was often aimed at the flaws within the system rather than the concept of organized religion itself. The parables, in essence, serve as a call to reform, a plea for authenticity and genuine leadership. Jesus' teaching encouraged a faith that was alive, dynamic, and responsive to the needs of individuals and communities alike.

As we explore these parables, it's essential to consider their relevance today. The same stories that challenged the religious leaders of Jesus' time still hold power to question and inspire modern believers and leaders within churches, synagogues, and mosques. The themes of humility, compassion, and true holiness are universal, and they continue to resonate in an age where organized religion often grapples with relevance and authenticity.

Furthermore, these parables offer a framework for understanding the relationship between personal faith and organized belief systems. They encourage individuals to pursue a personal, transformative connection with the divine that is informed, but not constrained, by institutional religion. This balance is crucial for a faith that is both sustainable and personally fulfilling.

It's crucial to consider how these narratives encourage self-reflection among religious practitioners. They prompt leaders and followers alike to examine their motives, practices, and the impact of their faith on the world around them. Do our actions reflect a sincere commitment to the principles we profess? Are we genuinely compassionate, or do we hide behind rules and roles?

Throughout history, these parables have sparked discussions around reform within religious institutions. From the Protestant Reformation to the modern-day movements for justice within the church, these stories have served as a catalyst for change. They remind us that the heart of religion should reflect the teachings of love, humility, and service that Jesus espoused.

In conclusion, the parables critiquing religious leaders offer a timeless exploration of the challenges faced by institutional religion. They highlight the need for a living faith that transcends regulations and rituals, inviting believers to seek a deeper, authentic relationship with the divine. Through these narratives, Jesus calls for a reform that begins within, urging religious institutions and individuals to align with the core values of compassion, humility, and love. Today, as in the past, these stories encourage us to reassess our faith practices and to strive for a spirituality that is both meaningful and genuinely reflective of the teachings of Christ.

Chapter 5:
Encounters with the Pharisees

In a time when religious norms were under intense scrutiny, Jesus' encounters with the Pharisees served as pivotal moments that questioned the boundaries of faith and authority. These interactions were more than mere debates; they were pointed challenges to religious orthodoxy and institutional power. Jesus, with a profound blend of wisdom and compassion, engaged in dialogues that unveiled the complexities of spiritual leadership. While the Pharisees upheld the letter of the law, Jesus delved into its spirit, emphasizing love, mercy, and authenticity over rigid adherence. It was in these moments that the essence of transformational faith emerged, urging a move from empty ritual to genuine connection with the divine. These encounters not only highlighted the tensions between Jesus and the religious elite but also offered timeless insights into the nature of true authority and the core of spiritual practice. By reflecting on these dialogues, one can discern the intersection of personal faith and organized religion, encouraging a journey of introspection and spiritual growth.

Analyzing Jesus-Pharisee Dialogues

In the robust dialogues between Jesus and the Pharisees, we witness a profound exploration of faith clashing with the constraints of institutional power. Jesus often engaged the Pharisees, the religious leaders of the time, in conversations that were both challenging and illuminating. Through these exchanges, Jesus laid bare the tension between genuine spiritual intent and the rigidity of religious legalism.

He adeptly used parables and pointed questions to reveal deeper truths, urging a shift from superficial adherence to the law to a heartfelt pursuit of righteousness. In doing so, Jesus wasn't merely critiquing the Pharisees; he was presenting a transformative vision for spirituality—one that prioritized compassion and authenticity over ritual and formality. By dissecting these dialogues, we can better understand how Jesus aimed to redefine religious authority, inspiring a break from traditional constraints in favor of a more expansive, inclusive faith. Experience these dialogues not just as historical confrontations, but as invitations to rethink the essence of religious devotion in our own lives.

Lessons in Religious Authority In the dialogues between Jesus and the Pharisees, we're offered a profound glimpse into how religious authority was both addressed and challenged. This interaction speaks volumes about the dynamics of power and belief within the context of first-century Judaism. Exploring these dialogues is not merely a theological exercise; it's a journey into the heart of what it means to hold spiritual authority and the responsibilities that come with it.

The Pharisees were well-versed in the law and took on roles as religious gatekeepers. Their influence was both respected and feared. Jesus' engagement with them wasn't just about disagreements on theology, but also a critique of how authority should be wielded in religious life. He often highlighted the tension between the letter of the law, which the Pharisees rigorously defended, and the spirit of the law, which he passionately advocated for.

Consider the instance when Jesus was questioned about healing on the Sabbath. The Pharisees strictly adhered to Sabbath laws, which forbade work. However, Jesus emphasized compassion over rigidity, suggesting that the Sabbath was made for man, not man for the Sabbath. Through this, he underscored a vital lesson: religious authority should serve people, enhance their spiritual journey, and alleviate their burdens—not add to them. This encounter with the Pharisees is a call to examine whether our spiritual practices align with the broader, humane principles they were intended to support.

Jesus often used parables to articulate his visions of authority. These stories transcended literal interpretation, urging listeners to delve deeper into understanding divine principles. By doing so, he subtly redefined the nature of authority from a top-down imposition to an internal, personal realization driven by empathy and compassion. Through narratives like the Good Samaritan, Jesus challenged the traditional boundaries set by religious authorities, inviting them—and his audience—to witness the divine in acts of love and kindness, which often defy institutional rules.

The dialogues reveal another critical aspect: the importance of questioning. Jesus' method wasn't simply to denounce but to provoke reflection. He asked questions that made the Pharisees, and indeed all who were listening, ponder their certainties and assumptions. This wasn't an undermining of authority, but a refinement of it—urging leaders to root their authority not in titles or positions but in wisdom, openness, and the pursuit of genuine understanding.

It's also noteworthy that Jesus didn't dismiss the Pharisees outright. His engagement with them suggests a recognition of their potential and importance. He seemed to strive toward a vision where authority was exercised with humility and was accountable to the broader community's needs, reflecting a leadership style that wasn't afraid of being challenged or corrected.

The Pharisees' responses to Jesus' teachings often exposed a vulnerability in traditional religious authority. It highlighted how rigid structures can risk becoming disconnected from the realities of life and the immediate needs of people. Jesus used these encounters as opportunities to teach that true authority doesn't resist change but rather adapts and grows with a deeper understanding of life's complexities.

In these engagements, we see the seeds of a transformative movement in religious thought. Jesus didn't come with a sword to cut down existing structures but with a conversation that encouraged a rethinking, a reimagining, and ultimately a renewal of how authority interacts with faith. It was a message urging leaders to move beyond rules and regulations into the realm of personal and collective transformation.

These lessons remain relevant today as we navigate our own relationships with authority within religious institutions. Jesus' conversations with the Pharisees remind us to ask: Do our practices and our leadership bring us closer to the fundamental tenets of love, compassion, and service, or do they act as barriers to those very ideals?

Ultimately, Jesus' interactions with the Pharisees weren't just historical confrontations—they invited a new paradigm of authority based on service and inner conviction rather than mere adherence to tradition. As we reflect on these lessons, we're called to not only examine the structures around us but also the structures within us, challenging us to live out a faith that is vibrant, questioning, and authentically engaged with the world.

Chapter 6:
Jesus' Views on the Law

In contemplating Jesus' views on the law, one is met with a figure who respects tradition yet challenges its rigidity, creating a dynamic tension that's both inviting and transformative. Jesus navigated Mosaic Law with a profound understanding, interpreting it not as a set of binding regulations but as a living testament meant to serve humanity. His approach was not about discarding the old but illuminating its spirit, emphasizing mercy over sacrifice, and love over legalism. This balance between adherence and innovation set him apart in a time of strict religious observance, as he sought to pierce through the veneer of tradition to expose the heart of divine intention. His teachings breathed new life into an ancient covenant, urging individuals to internalize the law in a way that transcended literalism and led to personal and spiritual liberation. This perspective not only invigorated his followers but also provoked the institutions to reconsider the true essence of their practices, making his views on the law as relevant today as they were two thousand years ago.

The Role of Mosaic Law

When examining Jesus' views on the law, the Mosaic Law holds a complex and nuanced role. While deeply rooted in the Jewish tradition of His time, Jesus approached these laws with a fresh perspective that often challenged the rigid interpretations of the religious authorities. His emphasis was not on the blind adherence to the law for its own sake but on understanding its true purpose: to cultivate a heart of compassion, justice, and mercy. Jesus frequently illuminated the spirit behind the law, urging His followers to see beyond the letter and embrace its transformative potential. By highlighting love and kindness as the ultimate fulfillment of the law, He provided a revolutionary perspective that encouraged a more heartfelt approach to spirituality, one that resonates with the seeker of truth in any era.

Jesus' Interpretations Versus Tradition In the discourse of Jesus' perspectives on Mosaic Law, the tension between adherence to tradition and the advent of new interpretations becomes markedly palpable. Jesus never outrightly dismissed the Mosaic Law; rather, he frequently reinterpreted its applications, often placing human need above legalistic adherence. This nuanced approach set him apart from traditional Jewish leaders of his time, illuminating the spirit of the law rather than the letter.

The spirit versus the letter is a theme that courses through many of Jesus' teachings. This was particularly evident in his response to the legalistic interpretations prevalent among the Pharisees. Jesus encouraged a deeper, more intrinsic comprehension of the law that aimed at internal transformation rather than mere outward compliance. His teachings, thus, were not a rejection of the law but an invitation to live it out with authenticity and purpose.

Consider the famous instance of Jesus healing on the Sabbath — an act that stirred controversy among those who adhered too strictly to tradition. The Mosaic Law dictated rest on the Sabbath, yet Jesus chose to perform acts of mercy. To him, this wasn't a breach of the law but its true fulfillment. The law intended for rest and restoration, and healing someone was the purest form of such an intention. It was a provocative reminder that love and compassion were at the heart of the Law, something tradition sometimes obscured.

Furthermore, Jesus' reinterpretation of the law often emphasized the relational rather than the ritualistic. He critiqued the Pharisaical approach of burdening people with heavy loads of tradition without fostering genuine spiritual growth. In his eyes, the Law was meant to guide people toward a more loving relationship with God and each other, rather than simply serve as a checklist of righteousness. His interactions were expressive of this belief, as he continually redirected focus from empty rituals to meaningful acts of love and justice.

Yet, understanding Jesus' interpretation demands an appreciation for context. He spoke to a community rich in traditions that had, over centuries, built complex interpretations of the Law. Jesus, therefore, respected the Law's historical depth, but he didn't shy away from challenging traditions when they clouded the divine intent. This balance is crucial; he wasn't repudiating tradition but seeking to reawaken its purpose in aligning human deeds with divine will.

His teachings on love, as encapsulated in the commandment to "love your neighbor as yourself," exemplify this paradigm shift. It suggested the Law was ultimately about relationships rather than regulations. Love transcended legalities, inviting a heart-driven observance that prioritizes compassion over compliance. This teaching, radical in its simplicity, dismantled barriers built by tradition, opening pathways to a more inclusive understanding of divine grace.

Many of Jesus' parables subtly embedded critiques of rigid traditionalism. These narratives, layered with meaning, often depicted scenarios where the outcast or overlooked were lifted up, and those entrenched in traditional righteousness missed deeper spiritual truths. Through allegory, Jesus revealed how tradition without transformation becomes mere performance; it loses the vibrancy of purpose and the authenticity of divine intent.

For an audience steeped in the practices of First-Century Judaism, Jesus' approach could have appeared daunting. Tradition provided a semblance of predictability and steadiness in a tumultuous world. Yet, Jesus' reinterpretation envisioned a dynamic, living faith that engaged with the heart of God's desires for humanity. This wasn't an easy transition, especially for those whose identity was tightly interwoven with established religious customs.

However, Jesus' teachings presented an aspirational vision that drew many towards a faith that broke through the confines of tradition, toward a broader, more enveloping embrace of God's love. This interpretive stance inspired followers to assess the Law not just as an external mandate but as an invitation to inward renewal. Such a perspective remains transformative, encouraging a shift from ritualistic obligation to intentional, love-driven action.

In conclusion, Jesus' readings of the Law versus traditional adherence crafted a narrative that speaks profoundly to both historical and contemporary audiences. His focus on the spirit of the Law reoriented discussions on faith from rigid formalism to vibrant relational dynamics. By doing so, he provided a framework that challenges us to consider how traditions serve the greater purpose of embodying love and justice, the core tenets of a life truly aligned with divine will.

Chapter 7: Community and Fellowship in Jesus' Teachings

Building a spiritual community was at the heart of Jesus' teachings, which often highlighted the nuances of fellowship distinct from formal religion. Jesus gathered a diverse group of followers who transcended social and religious boundaries, emphasizing inclusive love and service over rigid rules. It wasn't about constructing an institution; it was about crafting connections based on understanding, compassion, and shared purpose. Jesus taught that a true spiritual community thrives on mutual support and a collective pursuit of moral and spiritual growth, reflecting the divine within each person. Unlike organized religion, which occasionally risked being bogged down by tradition, His vision encouraged a living, breathing faith that evolves alongside the community. Through parables and interactions, Jesus illustrated how fellowship in faith glues people together, forming a network of relationships grounded in love and action, challenging us to redefine what it means to belong and to practice our beliefs in daily life.

Building Spiritual Community

In Jesus' teachings, building a spiritual community wasn't just about proximity or shared beliefs but about creating a vibrant fellowship centered on love, compassion, and collective growth. He envisioned a community where personal connections thrived over rigid structures, where the marginalized found a voice, and everyone felt included. Such a community, as Jesus illustrated, wasn't bound by brick-and-mortar confines or strictly adhered doctrines; rather, it was woven together through acts of kindness, empathy, and mutual support. By gathering disciples and engaging with followers outside conventional religious boundaries, Jesus demonstrated that spiritual communities lie in authentic relationships and shared missions. In his vision, the spiritual community is a living organism, evolving and adapting, fostering a sense of belonging and purpose beyond traditional religious formalities.

Distinction from Formal Religion Within the fabric of Jesus' teachings, we find a tapestry woven from threads of spiritual community that often stand in contrast to the formal structures of the religious institutions of His day. While Jesus frequently criticized the rigidity and sometimes hypocrisy found within formal religion, His vision of community emphasized authenticity and the transformative power of personal relationships. In many ways, His teachings encourage a departure from established norms, advocating for a deeply personal and relational spirituality that might be missed in traditional religious practices.

At the heart of this distinction is the idea that community, as envisioned by Jesus, isn't merely about gathering under a shared creed or within a physical temple. Rather, it's about creating connections that transcend those formal boundaries. This aligns with His message that "where two or three gather in my name, there am I with them" (Matthew 18:20). Such a principle defies the necessity of grand infrastructures or elaborate rituals, focusing instead on the intimate and immediate experiences of individuals seeking spiritual unity.

Jesus' interactions with various communities showcased His belief in the importance of internal spiritual development over external compliance with tradition. His encounters with people from different backgrounds, including tax collectors, sinners, and even the Pharisees, underscored a message of inclusion and personal transformation that wasn't contingent on one's standing in society or adherence to stringent religious codes. By focusing on the heart and the intention behind actions, Jesus proposed a more fluid and dynamic form of spirituality. This approach stood in stark contrast to the rigid formalisms that characterized much of the religious practice in His time.

One of the most compelling distinctions between the spiritual community envisioned by Jesus and formal religion is the emphasis on love and service. While institutional religion often prioritized adherence to rules and performing rituals, Jesus placed a higher value on the principles of love, compassion, and service to others. His parables and teachings consistently reinforced the idea that genuine faith is demonstrated through acts of kindness and treating others with respect and dignity. This message not only challenged the legalistic interpretations of the time but also invited followers to embrace a more profound, action-oriented faith.

This approach to community reflects a broader inclusivity that Jesus championed, which sometimes put Him at odds with established religious authorities. By inviting everyone—from the marginalized to the well-established—to participate in this spiritual journey, He broke down barriers that formal religion often upheld. His vision of community was one that embraced diversity, encouraged dialogue, and fostered mutual support, rather than division and exclusion.

Furthermore, Jesus' focus on inward faith rather than outward appearances posed significant challenges to the religious elite. In His denunciations of the Pharisees, He consistently warned against hypocrisy, emphasizing the danger of prioritizing rituals over genuine spirituality. Jesus' statements like "Woe to you, teachers of the law and Pharisees, you hypocrites! You give a tenth of your spices—mint, dill and cumin. But you have neglected the more important matters of the law—justice, mercy and faithfulness" (Matthew 23:23) reveal His concerns about the superficiality that can pervade formal religious practices.

The community building that Jesus advocated was not meant to create division between His followers and formal religious structures, but rather to bridge the gap between rigid doctrinal observance and living a life rich in spiritual abundance. This paradigm shift encouraged followers to seek a deeper connection with God through personal experience and communal support, rather than through hierarchical intermediaries or prescribed rituals alone. In this sense, the spiritual community was seen as a living organism, vibrant and responsive, rather than a static institution.

Moreover, the way Jesus modeled leadership within His spiritual community also differed significantly from that of many religious hierarchies. He exemplified servant leadership, where the greatest in the community was one who served others. This leadership by example shifted the focus from authority and control to empowerment and service, illustrating how true greatness lies in humility and dedication to the well-being of others. Such a model invites continuous engagement and participation from all members, rather than passive observance, fostering a more dynamic and responsive form of spiritual community.

In exploring Jesus' distinction from formal religion, it's also crucial to consider the cultural and historical context. The first-century Jewish religious landscape was characterized by a complex network of rituals, laws, and traditions that governed not only the spiritual lives of individuals but also their social and political interactions. It was into this intricate system that Jesus introduced His radical teachings of grace, forgiveness, and unconditional love. His vision, as a result, often contradicted and even directly challenged the dominant religious paradigms of His time.

Ultimately, the distinction Jesus made between spiritual community and formal religion invites reflection on the nature of faith itself. His teachings encourage a living faith, one that isn't merely bound to tradition for tradition's sake but is ever-evolving and deeply personal. This form of faith is marked by an unpretentious simplicity, grounded in love for God and others. It requires a willingness to listen, learn, and grow both individually and communally, with an understanding that genuine spiritual practice transcends the walls of any temple or church.

Through these distinctions, Jesus presented a transformative vision of community that's still relevant today. It calls believers to evaluate the essence of their faith and encourages the creation of spiritual communities that reflect inclusivity, service, and authentic connection. Jesus' approach wasn't to dismantle or disregard existing religious traditions but rather to fulfill and elevate them by emphasizing inward transformation and outward expressions of love. In recognizing these distinctions, spiritual seekers are invited to explore a path that both honors tradition and embraces innovation, continually rekindling a fervent hope for personal and communal renewal.

Chapter 8:
Jesus and Synagogue Practices

In exploring Jesus' interactions with synagogues, we're stepping into a realm where tradition meets revelation, where sacred spaces become stages for profound teachings. Jesus engaged with these community centers not just as a participant but as a transformative presence who challenged norms and redefined what communal worship could mean. This chapter unveils how Jesus, deeply rooted in Jewish practice, used synagogue gatherings as opportunities to illuminate and question interpretations of the law and religious authority. His presence within these walls wasn't merely that of a passive spectator but of an active reformer, engaging with congregants in a manner that was at once familiar and radically revolutionary. By examining his participation and teachings within these local assemblies, we garner insights into how Jesus valued the communal aspects of faith while simultaneously inviting deeper, more personal connections to the divine, challenging the status quo and inviting us to reconsider the spaces where spirituality unfolds.

Engagement with Synagogues

Engagement with synagogues was pivotal to Jesus' ministry, reflecting both his Jewish identity and innovative vision for faith practice. He frequented these communal spaces, not only to participate in religious activities but also to challenge prevailing interpretations and spark transformation. Imagine the energy as he stepped into a synagogue, weaving traditional worship with fresh insights, inviting both introspection and growth. His presence wasn't just that of a passive participant; he engaged actively, often speaking with profound authority that both captivated and confounded. Jesus drew upon scripture with a blend of reverence and radical reinterpretation, expanding perspectives while staying deeply connected with his roots. Through these synagogue encounters, he created ripples of change, encouraging individuals to look beyond rigid traditions and embrace a living, dynamic faith. By bridging the historical and the revolutionary, Jesus crafted a path that was both grounded in heritage and open to divine possibilities.

Understanding Jesus' Participation delves into the intricate relationship between Jesus and the synagogues of His time—a relationship marked by regular attendance, teaching, and moments of profound revelation. When we consider first-century Judaism, the synagogue was more than just a place of worship. It was a hub of community life, a center for learning, and a venue for discussing the pressing religious and social issues of the day.

Jesus, throughout His ministry, engaged deeply with these institutions, often using them as platforms to challenge prevailing religious norms and to introduce transformative teachings. His participation in synagogues offered Him the opportunity to connect with diverse groups, from devout Pharisees to curious onlookers, eager to hear His interpretations of sacred texts.

In many ways, Jesus' engagement with synagogues reflected His broader mission—a mission to reach the heart of Jewish tradition and open it to new revelations. By understanding His participation, we see a pattern of conscious connection, a desire to be both inside and outside the structures of his time. He respected the synagogue's role in community life, yet He did not shy away from questioning practices that, to Him, seemed more about ritual than genuine spiritual connection.

One notable aspect of Jesus' participation was his use of the synagogue as a space for teaching. The Gospels recount numerous instances where He read from the Scriptures and delivered teachings that often left His listeners in awe or confusion. His approach wasn't about dismantling tradition; instead, He sought to fulfill and expand upon it, pointing toward deeper meanings and more profound spiritual truths.

Consider the episode in the synagogue of Nazareth, where Jesus reads from the book of Isaiah. His declaration of fulfilling the prophecy startled many. It was not just His reading but how He interpreted it—it was transformative, promising liberation and a new vision of God's kingdom. Here, His engagement was more than participation; it was an invitation to see the old with new eyes.

Jesus' actions in synagogues also showed His flexibility in understanding religious practices. He spoke against rigid interpretations of the Sabbath laws and other regulations that he believed overshadowed genuine compassion and mercy. His presence often incited debate with religious leaders, sparking conversations that pushed the boundaries of conventional religious thought.

Synagogues provided Jesus with the public platform needed to dismantle the barriers between religious law and heartfelt faith. Through His participation, He neither entirely accepted established norms nor outright rejected them; instead, He reinterpreted those norms to align with His vision of God's will. Jesus sought to remind His audience that true worship stemmed from the intent of the heart rather than adherence to strict procedures.

Perhaps one of the most enduring aspects of Jesus' involvement in synagogue life was His ability to stir the hearts of individuals. His words and actions in these spaces resonated with those who were desperate for hope, for a Messiah who would bring clarity and truth amidst confusion. Those who listened to Him found in His teachings a bridge between the weight of tradition and the promise of an evolving understanding of faith.

As we examine Jesus' participation in synagogues, it becomes evident that He navigated a complex landscape—a landscape where tradition and spiritual progress could coexist. Through His teachings and presence, Jesus not only observed the practices of His faith but actively shaped them, inspiring his followers to see their traditions and institutions in a new light.

In synthesizing Jesus' engagement with synagogues, we see a reflection of His larger message: a call to spiritual awakening and sincere devotion. His active participation was a testament to His belief that existing religious practices, when approached with love and understanding, could lead to profound personal and communal transformation.

Chapter 9:
The Kingdom of God as an Alternative

The Kingdom of God, as envisioned by Jesus, offers a bold alternative to traditional religious structures, standing as a beacon for those yearning for spiritual authenticity. It's a concept that's both revolutionary and deeply inclusive, welcoming those who feel marginalized by the rigidity of established faiths. Jesus' teachings on the Kingdom paint a picture not of a distant realm, but of an ever-present reality, accessible here and now to those who embrace its ideals. Unlike institutional religion, which often prioritizes hierarchy and dogma, the Kingdom promotes values of love, justice, and compassion as its core tenets. This transformative vision challenges believers to re-evaluate their spiritual priorities, stirring a movement towards a faith rooted in communal harmony and personal connection with the divine. It's not about dismantling religion but rather transcending it, fostering a direct and profound relationship with God that empowers individuals to live out their highest values in everyday life.

Vision of the Kingdom

The vision of the Kingdom of God, as presented by Jesus, offered a radical departure from the religious institutions of his time. Imagining a realm not confined by walls or rituals, Jesus described a spiritual community marked by justice, compassion, and love—a place where societal hierarchies dissolved and each person had direct access to the divine. This was a living Kingdom, present in acts of kindness and selfless service, transcending traditional religious boundaries and emphasizing personal transformation over adherence to rote ceremony. Rather than a distant future promise, Jesus' portrayal of the Kingdom was an invitation to embrace a new way of life, one rooted in the here and now, challenging believers to cultivate an inclusive, equitable community reflective of divine will on earth. In essence, the Kingdom called for a revolution not in politics or geography, but in the hearts of individuals, urging a shift in perception from religion as an institution to faith as a lived experience.

Comparison with Traditional Religion offers a fascinating lens through which to view the "Vision of the Kingdom" as a transformative model that challenges age-old religious structures. The Kingdom of God, as Jesus spoke of it, forms a paradigm shift from the hierarchical and rule-based systems of traditional religion. Instead of rigid adherence to laws and rituals, the Kingdom envisions a realm grounded in spiritual principles that foster connection, compassion, and authenticity.

The traditional religious framework often emphasizes structure, ritual, and authority. In many ways, these systems were designed to provide social order and communal identity among believers. However, they can also institutionalize practices that risk becoming hollow, devoid of the very spiritual essence they aim to cultivate. Jesus' vision of the Kingdom subverts these expectations by emphasizing internal transformation over external conformity. He calls for a shift from outward religious displays to an inward journey of the heart.

This is not to entirely dismiss the value inherent in traditional religious practices; rather, it is to recognize a need for harmony between ritual and genuine spiritual growth. The Kingdom of God invites believers to transcend mere participation in religious activity and embrace a lived experience of faith characterized by love and justice. The traditional focus on compliance and dogma finds itself challenged by this Kingdom ideal, which prioritizes personal relationship with the divine and compassionate action.

In this way, the Kingdom of God critiques not only the religious status quo but also our understanding of power and authority. Traditional religion often places spiritual leaders in positions of control, sometimes leading to a dynamic where spiritual engagement becomes transactional—where piety is measured by adherence to visible norms rather than the cultivation of inner virtues. In contrast, the Kingdom is much less about control and more about empowerment, inviting each individual to be an active participant in their spiritual journey.

The contrast becomes particularly stark when examining how life within the Kingdom is organized compared to traditional settings. While the latter may prioritize hierarchy and status, the former embraces egalitarian principles. In the Kingdom, the first will be last, and the last will be first, a concept that disrupts accepted social and religious norms. This invites a decentralization of sacredness from specific spaces and rituals to the everyday moments of life, validating each person's experience as part of a divine tapestry.

Where traditional religion might be summarized as a way of maintaining divine favor or mitigating divine wrath through specific acts, Jesus' Kingdom reframes these motivations. It suggests that living under the rule of God is less about appeasement and more about embodying divine love and justice. The Kingdom vision suggests that God's rule is not oppressive but liberating, providing an entirely new motivation for spiritual practice: one rooted in freedom and love, rather than fear and obligation.

Moreover, the Kingdom of God critiques the transactional nature of many religious practices. Traditional religion sometimes treats faith as a bargain: perform a certain quota of good deeds, and in return, receive spiritual benefits. Jesus turns this idea on its head by suggesting that in the Kingdom, acts of love and charity are not bargaining chips but natural outpourings of a heart aligned with God's will. Such acts are genuine expressions of a transformed life, not calculated efforts to gain favor.

Consider the Pharisees, who often clashed with Jesus over interpretations of the Law. They embodied the rigidity and exclusivity that could creep into religious observance. Jesus' dialogues with them underscore how legalistic adherence can miss the point of the deeper moral imperatives of the Law, which are patience, love, and mercy. The Kingdom promotes inclusivity and grace, offering a spiritual community that transcends barriers of class, ethnicity, and religious background.

The community envisaged in the Kingdom is one of open-hearted fellowship, where relationships are prioritized over orthodoxy. This can be deeply unsettling for those accustomed to structured religious life. However, it also provides a liberating sense of belonging that's not contingent upon adherence to particular doctrines but on shared values of compassion and mutual respect. Rather than a closed circle of "us versus them," the Kingdom operates like a banquet where all are invited.

This new model of spiritual interaction posed by the Kingdom challenges traditional leaders and followers alike to consider the essence of their faith. It stirs us to ask whether our religious practices draw us closer to God and to each other, or whether they create barriers. The Kingdom of God is revolutionary in its simplicity—it invites individuals to enact their faith through daily acts of goodness and grace. Jesus' vision serves as both a measure and a call to authentic spirituality that is lived, not merely observed.

Finally, in comparing the Kingdom with traditional religion, one should appreciate the call for a dynamic, active engagement in the world, as opposed to static observance. This is a spirituality that is lived out in every interaction and situation, imbuing all aspects of life with sacred significance. The Kingdom model encourages us to move beyond the confines of labeled religion into a lived experience of faith where our values are evidenced by our actions.

Without negating the role traditional religion has played throughout history, Jesus' vision challenges us to reimagine the spiritual landscape. In the Kingdom's embrace of radical love and inclusivity, we're encouraged to build a world that reflects divine grace in action, challenging, and possibly transforming, the structures that have long shaped the religious experience.

Chapter 10:
Jesus' Critiques of Religious Hypocrisy

In his profound wisdom, Jesus held a mirror up to the religious practices of his time, yet what he revealed was as relevant today as it was then. He critiqued the hollow rituals that masked inner decay, pointing out that outward displays of piety often hid hearts untouched by true faith. Jesus challenged religious leaders who prioritized tradition over compassion and used their positions to wield power rather than nurture spiritual growth. His parables and teachings exposed the gap between appearance and reality, urging followers to seek authenticity in worship. This confrontation with hypocrisy was not merely a condemnation but an invitation to a deeper, more meaningful relationship with the divine. It highlighted the consequences for organized practice, emphasizing the need for sincerity and love as the foundation of spiritual life. His revelations beckon those trying to navigate their faith, encouraging an exploration beyond the facade into the sincere pursuit of truth and light.

Identifying Hypocrisy in Worship

In exploring the theme of hypocrisy in worship, it's apparent that Jesus didn't shy away from calling out the gap between appearance and true devotion. This section of the book shines a light on moments when Jesus' teachings pointedly addressed those who practiced religion outwardly while neglecting its spiritual essence. Imagine a scene where rituals are performed with precision but lack genuine love and humility—they become mere performances. Jesus emphasized authenticity and sought to peel away the layers of pretense, urging His followers to strive for inward purity over external display. Engaging with this critique challenges us to reflect on our personal religious practices and encourages an alignment of faith and action that is both sincere and profound.

Consequences for Organized Practice In the exploration of Jesus' critiques on religious hypocrisy, particularly through the lens of "Identifying Hypocrisy in Worship," we unearth profound implications for organized religious practice. Jesus' teachings often spotlighted the discrepancy between outward religious ceremonies and the inner spiritual truths these ceremonies were meant to represent. This dichotomy forced religious leaders and followers alike to confront the authenticity of their worship and the integrity of their spiritual lives.

It's crucial to understand that hypocrisy in worship, as identified by Jesus, wasn't merely about minor failings or occasional lapses in judgment. It was about a systemic flaw pervasive in organized religious practice—where form often eclipsed essence. Jesus challenged the ritualistic practices that had become disconnected from genuine spiritual pursuit and communal wellbeing. This critique was not an outright rejection of ritual or structure but rather a call for a revival of sincerity and purpose within established religious frameworks.

The consequences of these critiques reverberated through the Jewish religious institution of Jesus' time, and have continued to echo throughout religious history, initiating a process of self-examination within these institutions. Religious leaders had to reckon with the uncomfortable truth that their authority and traditions might be hindering, rather than helping, spiritual growth and communal integrity. This reckoning calls for a shift in focus from rigid adherence to rituals towards nurturing a more profound, personal connection with the divine.

What emerges from Jesus' critiques is an invitation to imagine religion not as a static entity but as a living, evolving organism capable of growth and renewal. For organized religions, this means re-evaluating the weight given to traditions and dogma in light of their ability to genuinely foster connections with the divine. It's about balancing the necessity of community structures with the spiritual freedom and authenticity that Jesus so ardently advocated.

The response to Jesus' critique demands a commitment to religious practices that are grounded in personal and corporate accountability. This means evaluating whether certain traditions encourage authentic worship or merely promote empty ceremonial compliance. Are religious communities fostering environments where inquiry and growth are welcome, or are they inadvertently stifling faith under the weight of misguided certainty?

This introspection extends to the leadership of congregations and religious institutions. Leaders are called to model a life of integrity and authenticity, bridging the gap between faith in action and belief in principle. In doing so, they can inspire congregants to pursue a faith that transcends the superficial and engages deeply with the spiritual and ethical teachings at the heart of their religious traditions.

Furthermore, organized religions are challenged to engage with the broader social context, addressing issues of justice, inclusion, and compassion as central expressions of their worship. Jesus' focus on the inward transformation must also inspire outward action—expressed through community service, social justice initiatives, and efforts to cultivate a compassion-driven society.

Engaging with Jesus' critiques invites a radical accountability that transcends mere observance and bets on transformation. It's about fostering dialogue within and beyond religious communities to ensure that the essence of religious practice remains aligned with its intended spiritual and communal outcomes.

Ultimately, the question posed to organized religion by Jesus' observations isn't solely about maintaining tradition or hierarchy, but about fulfilling the deeper aspirations of faith—a faith that elevates love, justice, and inward sincerity above mere ritual compliance. The future of organized religion hinges on its capacity to embrace this transformative journey, ensuring that its practices genuinely reflect the divine intentions they seek to honor.

Chapter 11:
Sacrifice, Ritual, and Faith

As we delve into the intricate relationship between sacrifice, ritual, and faith, we're confronted with a profound reconsideration that Jesus introduced in a world steeped in tradition. His vision wasn't merely a dismissal of the rituals but a transformation of their essence, calling for an internal rebirth over external adherence. Jesus, in his teachings, emphasized that true worship transcends the physical sacrifices, urging a movement towards sincerity in spirit and intent. This paradigm shift required a departure from ritualistic formalism and invited believers to foster a genuine connection with the divine. Such a reinterpretation challenged the very heart of organized religion, compelling followers to reassess whether their practices were mere gestures or reflections of a deeper faith. This idea of sacrifice, then, became less about material offerings and more about the surrender of the ego, a radical call to live with compassion and humility, embodying the essence of what it means to truly worship in faith.

Reevaluating Traditional Sacrifices

In the heart of the discussion on sacrifice, ritual, and faith, it becomes crucial to reconsider the role of traditional sacrifices through the lens of Jesus' teachings. The notion of sacrifice in ancient religious practices often centered around offerings meant to appease or gain favor from the divine. However, as we delve into how Jesus approached these longstanding customs, we find a transformative perspective urging believers to move beyond mere ritualistic acts. His teachings invite a deeper reflection on the essence of sacrifice as an internal, spiritual offering rather than purely external compliance. In this context, true sacrifice is reimagined not as the ceremonial slaughter of animals but as an authentic surrender of ego and material attachments, inviting a renewed focus on love, compassion, and genuine connection to the divine. This shift encourages a more personal and heartfelt engagement with faith, steering away from the rigidity of tradition and towards a practice that resonates with the ethical and spiritual core of Jesus' message.

Jesus' Concept of True Worship reverberates through the ages as a call for authenticity in spirituality and a reminder of the profound relationship between humanity and the divine. At the heart of this concept lies a revolutionary idea: that genuine worship isn't defined by elaborate rituals or costly sacrifices, but by the sincerity of the heart and a life aligned with love and justice.

Jesus' teachings often turned established religious norms on their heads, offering perspectives that were both radical and deeply rooted in a yearning for truth. During a period when traditional sacrifices were deemed necessary to appease God, Jesus challenged this view head-on. He didn't outright dismiss the rituals or invalidate the sacrificial system, but rather highlighted their limitations and potential for misunderstanding. He emphasized that actions devoid of love and genuine intention could become hollow.

Consider the instance when Jesus declared, "I desire mercy, not sacrifice." This wasn't merely a dismissal of traditional practices but an affirmation of something far deeper. In essence, Jesus noted that acts of mercy and compassion were the true sacrifices that God cherished. His message was simple yet profound: love and forgiveness are the ultimate offerings to God.

Jesus often had to confront the religious authorities of his time, who he believed had sometimes lost sight of the true essence of worship. It wasn't about grand displays of piety or the adherence to each letter of the law. Instead, the purity of one's intentions and the sincerity with which one lived God's commandments formed the true essence of worship.

In reevaluating traditional sacrifices, Jesus drew attention to the spirit behind the law rather than the law itself. This perspective caused quite a stir among the Pharisees and other religious leaders who held a literal interpretation of religious teachings. For Jesus, the transformation of the heart and mind was paramount. The external rituals should reflect an internal reality—a heart that is penitent, humble, and aligned with divine principles.

For many of his followers, this perspective offered liberation from the burdensome requirements that often left worshippers feeling inadequate or unworthy. By prioritizing the internal disposition over external rituals, Jesus invited people to experience a more personal and direct relationship with the divine.

Furthermore, his encounters and conversations with individuals from various walks of life further illuminate this understanding. From marginalized women to despised tax collectors, Jesus demonstrated that true worship was an expression accessible to all, not confined to a specific location or practice, but lived through one's daily actions and choices.

Jesus' discourse with the Samaritan woman at the well is particularly illustrative of his views. He spoke about a time when true worshippers would worship the Father "in spirit and truth." This envisioned future wasn't tied to a particular physical place, such as Jerusalem or Gerizim, but instead was concerned with authenticity and spiritual alignment.

The shift he proposed sparked significant reflection in both Jewish and emerging Christian communities. By moving beyond traditional locations and forms of worship, he emphasized that what mattered was how worship transformed the individual and ultimately, the world around them.

As we explore these concepts today, there's much to glean from Jesus' vision of true worship. In a modern world filled with its rituals and routines, his teachings challenge us to pause and reflect on whether our actions are aligned with the core tenets of compassion, mercy, and justice. Jesus invites us to evaluate the substance of our worship—whether it's genuinely transformative or merely a performance.

His focus on the heart resonates with the words of many spiritual leaders who have come after, echoing the timeless principle that love, justice, and authenticity form the foundation of true worship. Jesus did not seek to replace one set of rituals with another but aimed to recalibrate the focus back to what truly matters.

Thus, Jesus' teachings invite each individual to engage deeply with their faith tradition while also provoking broader questions about the nature of organized religion and its role in personal spiritual journeys. In today's context, where many seek a more personal spirituality outside institutional frameworks, his views provide both a challenge and an opportunity.

The journey toward true worship is one of introspection and personal transformation. Jesus' vision compels us to look beyond the superficial and to cultivate a deep connection with the divine, where love and justice are the cornerstone of our spiritual expression. As this understanding grows, it reshapes how we view both individual and communal faith practices, inviting a fresh perspective on what it means to truly worship.

Chapter 12:
The Legacy of Jesus and Organized Faith

The legacy of Jesus in organized faith is a complex tapestry woven from threads of his teachings, actions, and the ripple effects of his life. His approach was revolutionary, prompting early followers to rethink the essence of worship and community. While Jesus didn't outright dismiss religious institutions, he challenged their core, advocating for a faith unshackled from rigid traditions. This invitation to explore a deeper connection with the divine resonated through the centuries, shaping how religious institutions developed and adapted across time. He offered a spiritual paradigm that wasn't confined by walls of temples or synagogues but thrived in the heart of personal transformation and communal love. In the arc of early Christian thought, the echoes of his words invited believers to envision a faith where the spirit triumphs over rituals, laying the groundwork for a dynamic interplay between personal belief and structured religion, an interplay that continues to evolve even to this day.

Jesus in Early Christian Thought

Early Christian thought grappled with understanding the profound impact of Jesus' teachings on existing religious frameworks and institutions. His revolutionary ideas didn't merely challenge the spiritual status quo; they set the stage for a transformative movement that transcended the confines of traditional Judaism. Early followers, particularly in the burgeoning Christian communities, sought to reconcile Jesus' radical call for heart-centered spirituality with the structured practices of organized religion at the time. They saw him not as a rejecter of the law but as one who refined its essence, revealing a richer, more compassionate interpretation. His emphasis on internalized faith over rigid ritual inspired profound theological reflection and a reevaluation of religious priorities. This reimagining of faith as a living, relational experience laid the groundwork for what would evolve into a new religious identity, driving a wedge between mere adherence to tradition and the dynamic pursuit of spiritual truth. In this context, Jesus' teachings moved from being a set of revolutionary ideals to the cornerstone of theological exploration, which would shape the church's foundational doctrines and its enduring legacy.

Lasting Impact on Religious Institutions In early Christian thought, the legacy of Jesus had a profound and enduring impact on religious institutions, steering the ship of organized faith into uncharted waters. As Christianity began to differentiate itself from its Jewish roots, early followers of Jesus grappled with how to encapsulate his revolutionary teachings within the framework of organized religion. This was not merely an effort to preserve his message but a necessity to create a sense of community and structured beliefs for the rapidly growing number of adherents.

From the outset, Jesus' life and teachings posed challenges to the existing religious order. The temple, a central hub for religious and social life in Judaism, was reimagined through Christ's actions and teachings. Jesus critiqued practices that he viewed as hypocritical or not aligned with true faith. These critiques became fundamental in shaping how early Christians viewed religious institutions. They felt a calling to go beyond the rituals and formalities, seeking a more spiritual connection with the divine that transcended the limitations imposed by traditional religious practices.

Early Christian communities faced the task of defining what organizational structures would look like when Jesus himself had often spoken against the rigidity and corruption he saw in the religious leaders of his time. The First Council of Nicaea in AD 325, marking a pivotal moment for institutional Christianity, sought to address these challenges by establishing core doctrines and creating unity among believers. This council, while not directly influenced by Jesus' immediate teachings, was an embodiment of the struggle to align organized religion with his ethos.

However, Jesus' radical message of love, compassion, and justice wasn't meant to abolish institutions but rather to reform them from within. In grappling with how to keep this mission alive, early church leaders often found themselves balancing tradition with innovation, reassessing the fundamental purposes of religious gatherings, and redefining what it meant to belong to a faith community. They were mindful of retaining Jesus' core message in a way that was both accessible and meaningful for new followers.

Anchored in Jesus' teachings, these communities began to embrace a vision of inclusivity, promoting the idea that all were welcome, regardless of social status or previous beliefs. This was revolutionary for the time and laid the groundwork for the church's future expansion. By moving away from exclusivity, early Christianity offered an alternative to the more rigid caste systems that were pervasive in other religious structures, thereby appealing to a broader audience.

The structural development of church hierarchy, while seemingly in contrast with Jesus' more informal approach, was necessary for managing the growing number of converts and maintaining doctrinal coherence. Bishops and other church leaders emerged as key figures who were responsible for guiding and nurturing their congregations.

They faced the arduous task of ensuring that teachings remained true to the spirit of the gospel, even as cultural and societal influences threatened to alter the message.

Jesus' critiques of religious hypocrisy ignited a self-examination within institutions that sought to embody his teachings. A continual push for authenticity meant that those in religious authority were expected to live out the values they preached. This is evident in the writings of early church fathers like Augustine and Tertullian, who emphasized personal holiness and accountability within the framework of organized religion.

Moreover, Jesus' vision of spiritual equality challenged entrenched norms, prompting early Christians to reconsider roles of women, slaves, and the disenfranchised within the church. This perspective encouraged a radical reshaping of societal norms, offering an egalitarian approach that was countercultural yet deeply rooted in Jesus' message of universal love and service.

The influence of Jesus on organized faith also catalyzed the development of monastic traditions. Monasticism became a venue for those seeking to live out their faith with the intensity and devotion they saw modeled by Christ. These communities, rich in contemplation and service, acted as spiritual counterbalances to the institutional church, maintaining a focus on interiority and personal relationship with God.

The lasting impact of Jesus on religious institutions is also observed in how these entities have maintained a focus on service to others, echoing his call to love one's neighbor as oneself. Throughout history, churches have been central in providing education, healthcare, and welfare services, extending Jesus' healing mission well beyond the confines of liturgical life.

In today's context, the tension between institutional framework and spiritual liberation that reflected Jesus' early followers remains relevant. The question persists: how do institutions maintain their relevance without straying from the core message of their founder? Modern religious institutions continue to grapple with issues like inclusivity, social justice, and authentic witness to values taught by Jesus.

In conclusion, the legacy of Jesus in shaping organized religion is a tapestry interwoven with challenge and opportunity. While the inherent tension of staying true to his transformative message in an ever-changing world is substantial, it's precisely this dynamic that keeps faith communities alive, evolving, and responsive to the human longing for connection with the divine. The lasting impact of Jesus is not so much a finished chapter as it is an ongoing narrative, inviting each generation to engage with the wonder and depth of his teachings.

Conclusion

In our journey through understanding Jesus' perspectives on organized religion, we've navigated a complex landscape of teachings, traditions, and societal norms that defined first-century Jewish culture. Throughout the chapters, it's clear that Jesus possessed a deep commitment to the spiritual experience over the rigid structures that often dictated religious life. His teachings consistently revealed a message of transformation—urging believers to look beyond superficial rituals and embrace a more profound relationship with the divine.

Jesus often used metaphors, parables, and direct challenges to highlight the disconnect between external practice and internal faithfulness. It's not difficult to see how his critiques of the Pharisees and his actions in the Temple were less about rebellion and more about stirring a spiritual awakening. He advocated for a faith that was lived, breathed, and woven into the fabric of everyday life, unhindered by elaborate rituals or the limitations of institutional oversight.

Understanding the historical Jesus in his original context provides clarity on his teachings' intent. His life and words were marked by an insistence that faith was personal and transformative—a contrast to the pervasive religious formalism. His Sermon on the Mount, for instance, taught values and morals that transcend mere religious obligation, suggesting an ethical framework grounded in compassion and empathy. These teachings encourage followers to live in harmony with the core tenets of love and kindness, often challenging the religious authorities' entrenched norms.

The parables Jesus shared frequently critiqued religious leaders, urging them and others not to miss the heart of God's message through superficiality. These stories invited listeners to consider faith's essence rather than its facade. By portraying figures in the stories who transcended traditional expectations, Jesus highlighted the importance of a sincere, authentic approach to faith that could exist even outside organized religion's conventional boundaries.

Furthermore, Jesus' engagement with the law reveals his nuanced understanding of divine intent versus human interpretation. He didn't dismiss the law outright but offered interpretations steeped in grace and contextual sensitivity, acknowledging Mosaic Law's historical significance while urging its application to be measured against love's highest standards.

When Jesus spoke of community and fellowship, he showed how spiritual communities could exist parallel to, or independent from, the structure of formal religion. His vision of an inclusive community aligns with the Kingdom of God's promise, where the last become first and societal hierarchies dissolve in the presence of divine love. Jesus' reimagining of community dynamics serves as a catalyst for re-evaluating how modern religious institutions could function more inclusively.

The critiques of religious hypocrisy were among his most potent messages, pointing out how fervor in ritual could mask deeper spiritual deficiencies. These observations maintain relevance today, reminding us to examine the integrity of our faith practices continually. Hypocrisy in religion undermines authentic worship, and Jesus' pointed critiques motivate ongoing reflection for believers and institutions alike.

In Jesus' legacy, we see a profound impact on early Christian thought, reshaping religious institutions as we understand them. His teachings laid the foundation for a faith that resists legalistic traditions and authoritarian structures, favoring a direct and personal relationship with the divine. The diverse interpretations of his teachings in early Christianity reveal both the struggle and the profound desire to reconcile institutional religion with a dynamic spiritual life rooted in Jesus' insights.

As we conclude this exploration, let us recognize that Jesus' perspectives on religion invite an evolutionary approach to faith. They challenge religious structures to be adaptable and responsive, centered on the core principles of love, justice, and humility. In a world increasingly shaped by division and disparity, the timeless lessons derived from Jesus' views offer a roadmap for fostering unity and understanding in spiritual practice.

Jesus' vision was not to abolish organized religion but to infuse it with authenticity. Thus, we are left with a call to examine our path, ensuring that our spiritual endeavors align not just with religious identity, but with the eternal truths of compassion and grace. Our task is to integrate these insights and elevate our religious experiences, fostering communities grounded in sincere and transformative faith.

Appendix A: Appendix (if needed)

As we delve deeper into understanding Jesus' views on organized religion, this appendix serves as a reflective coda to expand upon the threads we've woven throughout this book. Here, we'll explore notions that couldn't find a place in the main text but still add richness to our discourse.

The Historical Context of Jesus' Teachings

One key area is the sociopolitical climate of first-century Palestine. The gospels, while spiritual in nature, echo the societal conditions of their time. Jesus spoke to a people under Roman rule, where religious leaders often collaborated with political powers. His criticisms frequently pointed toward the misuse of religious authority rather than the institutions themselves. Understanding this context helps readers perceive Jesus not just as a spiritual teacher but as a radical reformer challenging systemic inequities.

Interpreting Parables Beyond the Surface

The parables of Jesus can be seen as more than moral tales; they are incisive critiques of contemporary religious practices. For instance, the story of the Good Samaritan critiques existing racial and religious prejudices, calling followers to a higher standard of love and justice. By examining these stories with fresh eyes, one uncovers multifaceted lessons relevant to both personal spirituality and institutional practices.

The Ongoing Dialogue with Pharisees

Consider the dialogues with Pharisees, often mischaracterized as adversarial. While Jesus critiqued certain Pharisaical practices, these interactions were complex conversations on how adherence to the law could align with deeper spiritual truths. Rather than dismissing all Pharisaical traditions, Jesus sought to reshape understanding to emphasize compassion over legalism.

Reflecting on Spiritual Community

Finally, Jesus' vision of community wasn't about dismantling institutions but transforming them to resemble the kind of fellowship he modeled—one rooted in mutual support, love, and humility. His teachings stress the importance of spiritual interconnectedness that transcends hierarchical structures, nudging us toward a more inclusive approach to faith.

This appendix invites readers to reconsider preconceived notions about Jesus and organized religion. By exploring his teachings within their historical and cultural milieu, we gain insights into how faith can be practiced with authenticity and integrity, a pursuit as relevant today as it was in the days of the early church.

- Reflect on the cultural backdrop of the gospels.
- Interpret parables with a lens on social justice.
- Examine the Jesus-Pharisee dialogues for their depth.
- Envision a spiritual community grounded in love.

www.ingramcontent.com/pod-product-compliance
Lightning Source LLC
Chambersburg PA
CBHW030317100526
44585CB00014BA/956